Paul and Carolyn,

BECOMING A
GOD
MAGNET

All God's best,

STUDY & DISCUSSION GUIDE

BECOMING A GOD MAGNET

STUDY & DISCUSSION GUIDE

HARVEY KATZ

BELIEVE BOOKS
WASHINGTON, DC

BECOMING A GOD MAGNET—Study & Discussion Guide
By Harvey Katz

This study & discussion guide, based on *Becoming a God Magnet* by Harvey Katz © 2006, was written with contributions by Whitney Von Lake Hopler and James D. Craig.

ISBN: 0–9787428–0–X

Library of Congress Control Number: 2007907051

Cover design: *Jack Kotowicz, Washington, DC, VelocityDesignGroup.com*
Layout design: *Jen Anderson*

Believe Books publishes the inspirational life stories of extraordinary believers in God from around the world. Requests for information should be addressed to **Believe Books** at www.believebooks.com. **Believe Books** is a registered trade name of **Believe Books, LLC** of Washington, D.C.

Printed in the United States of America

CONTENTS

ACKNOWLEDGMENTS

I would like to thank Whitney Von Lake Hopler and James D. Craig for their work on this study and discussion guide. Each in their own way captured the essence of *Becoming a God Magnet,* and each brought new insights into how to best generate thought, discussion, prayer, and action for what will hopefully become new a generation of 'God Magnets.' I also appreciate the thorough and careful editing of the guide by Rebekah Young and Derek Axford.

BECOMING A GOD MAGNET STUDY & DISCUSSION GUIDE

HOW TO USE THIS GUIDE

This study guide is designed to help you apply the principles of evangelism that you have learned from reading *Becoming a God Magnet* and to start the work God is calling you to do – attracting people to the Gospel through His power at work in your life.

Whether you use this guide by yourself or as part of a group, it should lead you to a deeper understanding of how to share your faith with others. You can take the passion you feel for evangelism now that you've read *Becoming a God Magnet* and channel that passion into embracing God's call. Don't stop at just being inspired to share your faith. Start sharing!

GROUP STUDY AND DISCUSSION

This guide is intended to be used as part of a four session weekly program. It is organized in the same format as *Becoming a God Magnet* with an introductory part, a first part that focuses on how to identify the needs and desires inside people's hearts, a second part that emphasizes building Godly character and inviting the empowerment of the Holy Spirit, and a final part that deals with the many methods we can use to present the single most important message of all – the Gospel of Jesus Christ.

Each part contains three sections: Ask, Pray, and Act. The Ask section features questions for reflection and discussion, the Pray section features ways you can talk and listen to God about the questions you've just considered, and the Act section suggests ways to put the concepts you've learned into action. Group members should all have read *Becoming a God Magnet* in advance of participation in the program and should also make sure to read the applicable part of the discussion guide in advance of each session.

HOW TO GET THE MOST OUT OF GROUP DISCUSSION

Small groups have great potential to enhance and enliven our spiritual learning and growth. Like most group activities, however, this potential is only achieved when all agree on a few basic guidelines. Here are some suggestions:

- Take your turn. Small group discussion works best when all have a chance to make a contribution. This means being brief and succinct, staying on topic, avoiding lengthy illustrations or personal stories, and not speaking again until everyone else has had the chance to speak.

- Listen with an open heart and mind. The whole point in studying together is to learn from each other. Respect the thoughts of others even if you disagree with them.

- When you disagree, follow the advice of Ephesians chapter 4, which says to "speak the truth in love" (4:15), "to be humble, gentle, and patient with one another" (4:2), "and to speak only what is helpful for building others up according to their need." (4:29)

- Avoid speaking critically of others and keep whatever is said in the group of a personal nature within the group. The power of small group study comes from transparency, but this requires the protection of discretion and confidentiality.

- Come to the group prepared to learn, to encourage one another, and to grow together. Pray for your fellow group members and look for ways to help and encourage them during the week.

A WORD TO SMALL GROUP LEADERS

Even if you are only leading the group on one occasion, keep these guidelines in mind:

- To prepare, read the related chapters in *Becoming a God Magnet*, then work your way through the questions in the Ask section for the study you are leading. Highlight the portions that you don't want to miss in case your group is not able to get to all the questions in the guide during the time set aside for your meeting.

- Consider including some of the Pray section in a time set aside for group prayer.

- Encourage group members to put into action some of the suggestions contained in the Act section during the following week before the next session.

- Bear in mind that some of the questions in the Ask section will solicit a variety of viewpoints and stories. Help the group to remain open to the riches of the various perspectives around the circle.

- Good group discussion involves a healthy balance of give and take. Encourage each member to share their thoughts, but avoid pressuring those who are less talkative. Help generous contributors make room for the views of others. Ask members to address their comments to the entire group – not just you.

- Remain sensitive to time. If a particular question or topic sparks strong interest, allow the group to pursue it within reason. In some cases you may need to summarize and move on to the next question. Avoid totally irrelevant topics.

- Consider asking one or two group members to close the session in prayer, highlighting some of the issues discussed during the session.

INDIVIDUAL STUDY

Here are some suggestions for using this guide for an individual study of *Becoming a God Magnet*:

- Develop a regular time and place for your study each day or every other day.

- Try doing each study over the course of a week if you can.

- As you go through each section, read the relevant chapters in *Becoming a God Magnet* so the material will be fresh in your mind.

- Share what you are learning with others. Discuss some of the questions in the Ask section with a few fellow believers and see what they have to say.

- Ask a close Christian friend or prayer partner to hold you accountable to the plans you make for implementing the suggestions in the Act sections. Share your plans with them and ask them to check back with you within a specified time frame to see how well you have followed through.

- Some of the questions can be used as discussion starters with non-believing friends. For example, you could say, "I am reading a book that claims everybody 'worships' or is devoted to something in their lives. Do you agree? Can you think of how people do that?"

Get ready to see God do some exciting work in your life as you study *Becoming a God Magnet*. You may find yourself attracting people to God in a way you never imagined possible!

SESSION | 1

INTRODUCTION:

Have you ever thought of yourself as a "God Magnet?" No? You are definitely not alone. Many Christians believe that the task of drawing people to Christ is up to those with a special gift of evangelism. Most would agree that everyone needs Jesus and should have an opportunity to hear about Him, but somehow we feel God would never make that happen through *us*.

Evangelism shouldn't be a chore or something you dread. It can be something that just happens naturally as you live out your faith.

That's because your life sends a message to everyone around you. Like a powerful magnet, your life's message either attracts people to God or repels them from Him. If others can see God at work in your life, they'll be drawn to Him through you.

You don't have to worry that you don't have what it takes to successfully share your faith. God has already called you to the task and He will surely equip you. As it says in *Becoming a God Magnet*, "The truth is, God wants to use *all* of His children—even you—to reach other people with the Good News of Jesus Christ" (3).

Not only has God called you to share your faith, but He will also give you all the power you need to do it well. When you rely on the

Holy Spirit to work through you, you'll attract people to faith like a magnet, and there's no limit to what can happen!

Ask:

CONSIDER HOW YOU DO—OR DON'T—SHARE YOUR FAITH

- How have you tried to share your faith with people in the past? What happened as a result? How did you feel about what happened?

- What recent opportunities to share your faith have you neglected? Why did you avoid reaching out in those situations?

RECOGNIZE HOW SHARING YOUR FAITH MAKES YOU FEEL

- When you miss opportunities to share your faith, do you feel guilty? If so, does that guilt make you more or less likely to share your faith in the future? Do you think God would want you to feel guilty? Why or why not?

- What fears do you need to overcome to start sharing your faith more often?

- Consider the fact that God isn't nearly as concerned about how many people you successfully lead to Jesus as He is about seeing you simply be faithful in reaching out to people with the Gospel message. How does that knowledge take pressure off you and free you to share your faith more?

- When you share your faith but people don't seem interested, do you take that as a personal rejection? What do you imagine they may be thinking of you, and why does that bother you?

- If someone you love dearly, such as a family member or close friend, were to end up separated from God for eternity even though you did all you could to reach that person, how would you feel, and why?

- When you share your faith and people respond positively, do you see that as a sign of God's blessing on you? Why or why not?

- If a loved one you've been trying to reach for many years but nearly given up on finally surprises you by coming to faith, how would you feel, and why?

- Have you ever tried to push, manipulate, or force someone into coming to faith? If so, why did you try so hard despite their resistance?

- Have you ever made just a minimal effort to share your faith and seen a dramatically positive result? If so, did that experience make you more or less likely to put your best effort into reaching people with the Gospel?

Relax:

- According to 1 Corinthians 3:6, 7, who bears the ultimate responsibility for someone coming to Christ? How can this help us when we think about our fears and past failures in drawing others to God (21, 22)?

- How does *Becoming a God Magnet* describe our part in bringing people to Christ? What will this require (22)?

- Why is it possible for us to relax in sharing our faith (24)?

- Why is it much easier for people to seriously consider what you have to say if you're calm and confident rather than argumentative and defensive?

DISCUSS PEOPLE YOU WOULD LIKE TO REACH

- Talk with others in your group about specific people you know who haven't yet come to faith in Christ – family members, friends, co-workers, neighbors, and others. Let your discussion jumpstart your thinking with creative ways on how to build closer relationships with those people.

Pray:
EMBRACE THE CONFIDENCE GOD OFFERS YOU

- Read the Great Commission (Matthew 28:18-20) and meditate on it, asking the Holy Spirit to help you embrace the call personally.

- Ask God to help you overcome unhealthy emotions like fear and guilt when you think of sharing your faith. Invite the Holy Spirit to renew your mind so you can view evangelism from God's perspective and become genuinely excited about it. Pray for God to give you the confidence you need to share your faith with anyone at any time.

- Remember that it's God – not you – who does the work of saving people. Ask God to help you relax and trust Him to work in the lives of everyone you're trying to reach for Him. Read the Parable of the Sower (Mark 4:1-9, 13-20) and imagine yourself sowing seeds of faith when you reach out to others. Pray for the peace you need to simply be faithful to minister to people as God leads, and leave the results up to Him. Ask God to free you from any pressure you feel to achieve certain results when you share your faith.

- Pray for the ability to see yourself as God sees you and understand that your success or failure when you share your faith won't ever make God love you any more or less than He already does.

INVITE GOD TO GIVE YOU OPPORTUNITIES TO SHARE YOUR FAITH

- Ask God to make you aware of specific people with whom He would like you to share your faith. Accept God's call to reach out to those people. Pray for the wisdom to recognize when and how you should connect with them. Ask God to open their hearts to receive His truth at the right time so that this truth will set them free.

- Pray with some other believers regularly so you can all intercede for the people God is currently leading each of you to reach.

Act:
GET READY TO REACH OUT

- Write down the names of people God has brought to your mind in your prayer times about sharing your faith, and write down the specific ideas you've received for how best to reach out to them. Then begin building relationships with them.

- Keep a prayer journal to notice how often God helps you and let that knowledge build your trust in Him to help you evangelize. Use your journal to keep track of how God answers your prayers for the people you're trying to reach.

START CONNECTING WITH PEOPLE GOD BRINGS YOUR WAY

- Don't be afraid to reach out to people you don't know. The next time you encounter someone who seems to need encouragement (such as a mom struggling with a toddler at a restaurant, a person who's lost and asks you for directions, a store cashier who's upset after dealing with a rude customer, or a disabled person working hard to get around in a wheelchair) offer that person a smile and any practical help he or she might need. If a conversation results, ask the person if you can pray for his or her needs.

- Be patient as people begin to open up to you about their spiritual journeys. Don't rush them to make a decision about Jesus before they're truly ready. Give them plenty of time and space to work through all the issues they need to deal with so their faith will be genuine.

- Resolve any conflicts you may have with any of the people God is leading you to try to reach. Rely on God's help to forgive people who have wronged you, and ask people you have wronged to forgive you. Do your best to reconcile so nothing will stand in the way of your relationship with each other and God.

- Practice telling people how God is currently at work in your life, so that it becomes a natural part of your conversations. Don't stop short of mentioning God if it relates to something you're discussing with others. Realize that God will often sow the seeds of faith in people's lives simply by having you call His everyday work to their attention.

- Make a habit of asking people questions that will naturally lead them to thinking more about how God may be working in their own lives. For example, if someone you know is searching for a new job, ask how he or she is trying to discover God's purposes. Or, if someone you know is experiencing a broken relationship, ask how God's love has been a source of comfort. You can also share with them how God has met your needs through answers to prayer and offer to pray for their situations of need that they may have described to you.

IDENTIFICATION:
Speaking to the Heart

Before you can successfully share your faith with other people, you need to get to know them well. *Becoming a God Magnet* points out that, "We cannot reach others for God unless we can truly speak to them by identifying or empathizing with who they are and with what might be the cry of their hearts" (25).

Once you discover the needs and desires inside people's hearts you'll be able to help them find fulfillment in God, through Jesus.

Ask:
CONSIDER WHAT IDOLS PEOPLE WORSHIP IN THEIR LIVES

- How does *Becoming a God Magnet* define idolatry (27)? Do you agree or disagree? Can you give a specific example of ways in which people set up idols in their lives? (see Colossians 3:5)

- What happens when people worship or devote themselves to something other than God (28-31)? How can this block people's hearts to God's love flowing through their lives?

- Discuss the ways that people you know try to find fulfillment apart from God. Do they turn to food, alcohol, sex, gambling, excessive work, too much television, or other addictive or escapist behaviors? Think about each one of the key people you sense God leading you to try to reach, and identify how they may be looking in the wrong place to get their needs and desires met.

BUILD RELATIONSHIPS OF TRUST

- Consider how the suffering you've gone through in your own life gives you compassion for people who are going through similar struggles. How have your challenging experiences opened doors for you to minister to others? How can you encourage people who are suffering in ways you once suffered yourself?

- When people don't respond as you hoped to your efforts to share your faith with them, are you annoyed? Are you tempted to give up and move on when people take too long to make progress spiritually? If so, what might help you to be more patient with them (34, 35)?

- Think about the last few times you've judged or criticized someone. Can you honestly say that you knew that person well, or is it possible that you made some assumptions about him or her?

- Why is it difficult to accept people as they are – faults and all–and why is it so tempting to try to change them?

- Discuss some practical ideas for how you and others in your group might demonstrate unconditional love to some difficult people in each of your lives. (Try to avoid naming names.)

TRUST GOD TO LEAD YOU

- Have you ever had an experience where the Holy Spirit prompted you to speak to someone or do something for him or her? Describe what happened.

- Have you ever tried to plunge ahead with an effort to share your faith on your own, without relying on the Holy Spirit's guidance? What happened?

- What does it mean, practically, to rely on the Holy Spirit to lead you as you share your faith? Explain how Proverbs 3:5-6 provides the wisdom you need to let the Holy Spirit guide you as you pray for and win others to Christ (43, 44).

- What does it mean when *Becoming a God Magnet* warns us against trying to play "Junior Holy Spirit"? What should we do instead (50, 51)?

- Why do you think that praying for people to come to faith is more effective than winning arguments with them about faith?

RESPECT PEOPLE'S BOUNDARIES

- According to *Becoming a God Magnet*, what are people's "spiritual boundaries" (53)? How can we ask permission to enter their personal space (53-55)? Have you ever done this or failed to do this? What happened?

- What are some types of personal boundaries you should be careful not to cross when you're trying to share your faith with someone with whom you haven't yet built a trusting relationship? Think about a time recently when someone crossed one of your boundaries. How did that make you feel?

- What are some of the things you can keep in mind in order to demonstrate sincere love and win people's trust as you listen to them (34, 35)?

READ PEOPLE'S SPIRITUAL BAROMETERS

- How can you read people's spiritual barometers to learn more about where they are with God? What types of cues might they give you?

- How does *Becoming a God Magnet* describe the "Unconvinced" compared to the "Inquirers" (57-60)? How should we respond to them?

- How can we identify "Seekers"? What are some of the things we need to bear in mind when dealing with them (60-62)?

- Can you give an example of a person you know who fits into one of these three groups? (Unconvinced, Inquirers and Seekers) How could you begin to reach them?

- What are some of the things that you should pray for people who are without God (37)?

- Discuss your personal spiritual journey with others in your group. What stages did you go through? How long did each one take? Who helped or hindered your progress at each stage? What did they do that was helpful? How might you use the knowledge you've gained from your own experiences to approach other people who aren't as far along as you on their spiritual journeys?

Pray:
SEEK GOD'S HELP

- Ask God to give you the wisdom you need to discern the deepest needs and desires of each person with whom you're trying to share your faith. Pray about each person individually, letting the information you discern about that person guide your prayers.

- Pray for opportunities to reach out to people who are suffering in similar ways to what you've experienced in your own life.

- Ask God to ignite a sense of curiosity in you as you relate to other people, so that you become genuinely interested in learning all you can about them.

- Pray for the ability to view people simply as individuals to love instead of projects to work on. Ask God to help you love people unconditionally. Invite God to pour His love through you to other people.

- Humble yourself before God, giving up your assumptions about how to best reach people and asking Him to show you specific ways to intercede for them. Trust God to reveal when and how to talk with each person about Jesus.

DISCERN PEOPLE'S BOUNDARIES AND SPIRITUAL BAROMETERS

- Ask God to give you the wisdom you need to discern where people currently are in their relationships with you and with God as you talk with them.

INTERCEDE FOR PEOPLE

- Choose some Bible verses that pertain to certain people or situations, and apply those verses personally to your prayers for them by reading the scriptures back to God while you pray about those people or situations.

- When people share their needs with you, ask if they would like you to pray about those needs. Then pray right there with them.

- Invite the Holy Spirit to pray through you as you pray for other people, since God is the only One who can see inside people's hearts to know what they truly need.

Act:
BUILD MEANINGFUL RELATIONSHIPS

- Learn to listen more than you talk. When you're involved in a conversation, give the other person your full attention and guard against being distracted or thinking of what you're going to say next. Make eye contact and let your body language show your interest in what he or she has to say. Listen carefully and respectfully, even if you don't agree with what the person expresses. Repeat back, in your own words, each key point that the person makes so he or she can clarify if necessary. Wait until the person is truly finished before responding.

- Build meaningful relationships with the people you want to reach. Be willing to invest the time and energy needed to build those relationships.

OFFER UNCONDITIONAL LOVE

- Offer love with no strings attached. Let people know that you'll still care about them even if they don't agree with you or fit into your agenda.

WRITE DOWN INSIGHTS

- Write down the insights God gives you about the hearts of people you're trying to reach. Share some prayer requests with other people you can trust to help you intercede for those for whom you're praying.

PAY ATTENTION

- Be sensitive to how the Spirit leads you as you talk with people about the Gospel. If you have a sense of God's peace, then proceed. But if you sense God's restraint, stop and wait for His better timing or His change of direction.

- Respect people's personal boundaries when sharing your faith so they don't feel threatened or pressured. Rather than jumping in with too much too soon, earn their trust over time.

- Pay attention to the cues people give you that indicate how ready they are to respond to the Gospel. If they don't show any interest, don't push. Be patient and sensitive as you watch for a better time. Feel free to ask them open-ended questions to encourage them to think more about spiritual matters, but be gentle when doing so, and don't keep asking if they change the subject.

REMEMBER THAT LOVE IS MORE PERSUASIVE THAN ANY ARGUMENT

- Avoid arguments. Simply state what you believe quietly and confidently, and show respect for what others believe, even when you disagree with their beliefs. Remember that others will likely be willing to listen and seriously consider your beliefs if you're not combative.

- Make it a high priority to establish loving relationships with people you meet, and stay sensitive to where they are in their growing relationships with you and with God.

SESSION | 3

PREPARATION:
You Are A Life Message

People pay more attention to the way you live your life than they do to the words you speak to them. Your life communicates a message to everyone you encounter, and if you want your evangelism efforts to be successful, your life should reveal your faith loud and clear.

If we are going to become God Magnets, our lives need to have the power of attraction. People we meet will want to see something that's worth having, something that draws them to us. We must ask ourselves—if we are a "life message"—what is that message?

"The importance of building godly character and of being empowered by the Holy Spirit cannot be overstated," we read in *Becoming a God Magnet*. "We need both to be ready to effectively share the Gospel" (67).

Ask:
WHAT IS YOUR LIFE MESSAGE?

- Is your life telling a message to others about your relationship with God, His faithfulness to you, and your trust in Him? Is it attracting people to God? Or is your life giving the impression to others that you are out of control and unstable in all your ways?

TRUST GOD WITH *ALL* OF YOUR LIFE

- Are you honestly trusting God to lead your decisions in every part of your life, or are you holding onto control over certain aspects of your life? If you're reluctant to trust God in certain areas, which areas are they, and why is it hard for you to let go? What might help you release control over those parts of your life and start trusting God to guide you fully?

- How do you address the fears of those who think repentance will make them into fanatics or crazy people? (74, 75)

- Why is it misleading to suggest that becoming a Christian is a formula for success? (75)

LEARN FROM SUFFERING

- What is the purpose of "the wilderness experience" in our lives and what does God do when we are there? (78) Have you ever experienced this? Please explain.

- How should we respond in our wilderness situation? What happens if we don't respond this way (79)?

- When you go through suffering, what are some specific ways you can trust God in the process to inspire others to trust Him during their own times of suffering?

LEARN FROM SIN

- How can you pursue God's healing when you are struggling with sin? When you experience this kind of healing, how can this help you point others toward the hope that only God can give?

DEVELOP GODLY CHARACTER

- How does God prepare our lives to be "God Magnets"? (Hebrews 12:13)

- What does it mean to "make straight paths for our feet"? (82)

- It has often been said, "While God accepts you as you are, He loves you too much to leave you that way." Have you ever used God's unconditional love as an excuse not to change, despite knowing deep down that you should change a certain attitude or behavior? Does it help you to see God's call to grow in holiness as a loving call?

- Which areas of our lives does God often begin to work on first? Why? Has this been your experience? (83. 84)

- Are you drawn more to people who display strong character, or magnetic charisma? Which is more important and why?

- Why do you think God uses ordinary people to accomplish extraordinary things? Discuss someone you know who isn't outwardly impressive, yet still accomplishes impressive things for God's kingdom. What can you learn from that person's example?

- Can you think of one area in your life where you need to make straight paths for your feet? Ask God to show you one crooked place in your life of which you are not aware. If you need help to get started, prayerfully read Galatians 5:19-23 or Ephesians 4:25-5:21. How and when will you deal with the issue that God speaks to you about?

- If the group is a large one, break into smaller prayer groups of two or three when you get to the Pray section and ask the others to hold you accountable for your response to the questions above.

INVITE THE HOLY SPIRIT TO EMPOWER YOU

- The Bible says that it is impossible for us to bring anyone to Christ. This is actually God's job, not ours. As *Becoming a God Magnet* declares, "If you have learned anything from this book…it will be that without the power of God, you can do nothing!" (103).

- What role has the Holy Spirit played in your journey toward faith in Christ?

- Do you know someone whose life is literally overflowing with God's Spirit? What is that person like?

- Have you ever experienced a time when God spoke to you clearly and revealed something to you through the Holy Spirit? What happened?

- Why is it vital for the Holy Spirit to empower you as you try to share your faith with someone? What are some specific ways that you need the Holy Spirit's help as you reach out? Think back to a time when you may have tried to evangelize someone without the Spirit leading you. What happened as a result? Now remember a time when you may have seen a Spirit-led breakthrough while you were sharing your faith. What happened, and why would that not have been possible without the Spirit's help?

- What is the difference between being saved and being filled with the Holy Spirit? Why are both necessary to fulfill God's purposes for your life?

- If you haven't prayed to receive the Holy Spirit, why are you hesitating? What might help you overcome your fears so you'll be ready to receive this gift from God?

- Do you struggle with any unbelief, fear, or unconfessed sin that may be blocking you from receiving the Holy Spirit? Discuss specific issues that people might have which are barriers to this experience.

Pray:
REPENT

- Repent from trying to run your own life and give God control over every aspect of it. Invite God to transform your character so that you become more and more like Jesus, and other people can recognize Him at work in you and be drawn to Him.

- Humble yourself before God, meditating on His awesome power. Express your gratitude to God for reaching out to you and working in your life. Ask Him to regularly remind you of how everything you have – even your next breath – is a gift from Him.

LET GOD REFINE YOU

- Pray about each character trait with which you currently struggle (such as honesty or courage), and ask God to help you develop strong character in each of your problem areas.

- Ask the Holy Spirit to renew your mind so you can get rid of negative attitudes and thought patterns that don't align with God's Word. Pray for the Spirit to fill your mind with positive, truthful thoughts.

- Pray for the wisdom, courage and strength you need to obey God in every decision you make – especially when you face temptation.

- Ask God to help you value character over charisma, just as He does. Pay more attention to the type of person you truly are on the inside than just the image you project to others.

EMBRACE GOD'S GIFTS WITH GRATITUDE

- Acknowledge that without God's power helping you, you can't accomplish anything. Thank God for the multitude of ways He helps you every day.

- Ask God to fill you with His Holy Spirit and to evangelize people through you. If you don't recognize signs of the Holy Spirit in you right away, don't worry or be self-conscious. Instead, simply keep your thoughts focused on Jesus and worship Him, trusting that God will definitely answer your prayer.

- Confess anything that may be blocking the Holy Spirit's work in your life, such as unbelief, fear, or sin. Ask God to help you overcome those challenges so you can grow closer to Him. Thank God for giving you forgiveness and the grace you need to grow.

Act:

GROW IN HOLINESS

- Schedule regular times to read, study, and meditate on the Bible, allowing its truth to transform your thinking.

- Break your bad habits by replacing them with good habits. Tackle one habit at a time, such as keeping your word if you have been unreliable, being honest with people if you have exaggerated the truth, and showing diligence at work if you have not been a hard worker. Rely on God's help throughout the process so others can see that they can rely on His help in their own lives.

- Find several people whose spiritual maturity you respect, and ask them to help hold you accountable as you go through the process of developing stronger character.

- Welcome God's discipline when it comes, trusting that He is fulfilling His good purposes in your life.

- Instead of worrying about impressing others with your natural abilities or credentials, focus on pleasing God by becoming the kind of person He wants you to become.

RELY ON GOD'S POWER

- Stop trying to share your faith on your own, apart from the Holy Spirit's help. Rely on God's unlimited power rather than your own limited power.

- Whenever you sense the Holy Spirit leading you to share your faith with someone, don't hesitate to approach that person. When you don't understand the ways in which you sense the Holy Spirit leading you to share your faith, or even if they seem outrageous to you, go ahead and obey the Spirit's leading. Trust that He knows best how to reach each person and that He will bless your efforts if you act on His guidance.

SESSION | 4

PRESENTATION:
One Message, Many Methods

Now that you're ready to present the Good News to other people, you have many possible methods for sharing the one life-changing Gospel message. You can look forward to God leading you in exciting ways as you consider the three basic questions: "What to share? When to share? How to share?"

Ask:
CONSIDER YOUR FOCUS

- What are the two things that we are responsible to do in evangelism (127, 128)? If we do these things, will everyone respond positively? Why or why not (128, 129)?

- Have you been investing your life in eternal purposes? How can you change the way you spend your time and energy to be better able to pursue what matters most and let go of whatever isn't truly important?

- As you think about the circle of relationships you currently have, what interests do you have in common with various people? How can you use those shared interests to build closer relationships with them?

- What type of behavior should we avoid when we share the Gospel with other people (131)? Why?

- How can humor help you overcome this problem (132)?

- What sort of preparation might help you to relax and avoid getting too intense when you share the Gospel with someone? Do you need to be more confident of your message, more comfortable talking about your faith, or better able to handle rejection graciously? Discuss how you can make these concrete preparations.

OVERCOME BARRIERS

- What is the key to sharing Christ with the people God brings across our path (141-146)? How do we put it into practice?

- What qualities do you find most attractive in people, and what qualities do you find most annoying or offensive? In what ways have these biases caused you to avoid building relationships with certain people in the past?

- Recall a time when you hesitated to reach out to someone who seemed to need the love of God. What stopped you from reaching out to that person? If you ever meet that person again, how might you overcome your hesitancy and reach out anyway?

DISCUSS ETERNAL LIFE

- Why is it sometimes awkward or frightening to discuss death with other people? What might make you feel more comfortable about bringing up the subject? (148)

- Briefly describe the three things that people must understand and act upon to receive eternal life (153).

- Why is it important to pray with people when they want to accept Christ? How does *Becoming a God Magnet* suggest that you should go about it (154)?

• Read 1 Corinthians 9:19-23. What does it mean to "present Christ in the context of those who were listening" (155)? How can this apply to people you know?

SHOW HOW THE GOSPEL IS RELEVANT

• How did you first hear the Gospel yourself? Was it presented in a way that truly reached your soul? Why or why not?

• What keeps some people from understanding how the Gospel relates to them personally?

- How can we present the Gospel in "culturally appropriate" ways like Apostle Paul did to the people of his day? (158)

SHOW HOW THE GOSPEL IS REAL

- What are the five reasons given in the book that help us know that God's Word is true (161-163)? Which of these five reasons is most convincing to you personally? Why?

- How can you overcome the popular notion that truth is merely relative and instead show people that the Gospel's truth is absolute and universal? (161-165)

SHOW HOW THE GOSPEL IS RELATIONAL

- Explain how Christ has restored our relationship with God (justification) and what this means for our daily lives (sanctification) in a way a non-believer could understand (168-170).

- Why do people first need to establish a right relationship with God through Jesus in order to enjoy healthy and fulfilling relationships with others?

- Our reconciliation to God through Jesus changes our relationships with each other. How does this happen? (170-173) Share an example of how you've experienced this in your own life.

SHARE YOUR PERSONAL TESTIMONY

- Has anyone ever shared his or her personal testimony with you? If so, how did hearing the story of how that person came to faith inspire you to seek more of God?

- Have you ever shared your personal testimony of how you came to love God? Why or why not? If you have, what happened as a result? If you haven't, how might you overcome your fears to start telling your story?

- At this point, it would be helpful for two or three volunteers from the group to briefly share their testimonies. Others should be thinking about how to share their own unique stories, to be ready for when the opportunity next presents itself.

CONSIDER RESOURCES THAT CAN HELP YOU SHARE THE GOSPEL MESSAGE

- What resources (books, tracts, CDs, videos, etc.) might you use to help you present the Gospel?

- Share examples with the group of any situations in which certain resources helped you lead someone to Christ.

DISCUSS HOW TO BEST ENGAGE PEOPLE

- What attitude do your non-Christian friends have toward Christianity? Why?

- What was your attitude toward Christianity before you became a believer? What sorts of ideas or experiences shaped this attitude?

- *Becoming a God Magnet* mentions raising your "banner of faith" (177). What does this mean (176-178)? How do you feel about it? Do you do this now? If so, do people respond?

- When people indicate that they want to explore their faith further, what worship services, group meetings, events, or courses might you invite them to attend at your church or elsewhere?

- Why do you think people sometimes stop reaching out to those with whom they've shared their faith once they become Christians? Why is it important to not just lead people to salvation, but also to disciple them so they can grow in their faith?

Pray:
INVITE GOD TO WORK THROUGH YOU

- Ask God to help you discern exactly what to share, when to share, and how to share with each person. Pray for the wisdom you need to approach every conversation in the right way.

- Pray for the ability to remain passionate and focused as you present the Gospel, no matter how people react.

- Ask God to help you be bold in sharing your faith.

- Pray that God will help you be open to building relationships with whomever He leads you to reach with His love – especially people you wouldn't naturally choose to befriend.

- Ask God to give you the courage you need to broach the subject of death with people when you're discussing their spiritual journeys.

- Pray for the wisdom you need to show people how the Gospel relates to their individual lives.

- Ask God to help you explain why the Bible presents absolute truth to all people. Pray for the courage you need to counter the popular notion of relativism with biblical truth.

- Invite God to work through you as you try to show people how a right relationship with God will lead to healthy and fulfilling relationships with others.

- Ask God to inspire you to create your personal testimony and learn how to communicate it well to others.

ASK GOD TO GUIDE YOU

- Pray that God would inspire you in choosing the right resources for each individual with whom you are sharing.

- Ask God to help you refrain from arguing with people as you discuss their spiritual views. Invite God to give you the gentleness, patience, and humility you need to minister effectively with all people, especially those with whom you disagree.

- Ask God to direct you as you try to help new believers grow in their faith.

Act:
AVOID ASSUMPTIONS

- Don't assume that people already know the Gospel. Be willing to explain it to them. Give them time to process the message on a personal level.

STAY FOCUSED AND PASSIONATE

- If people criticize you as you try to share your faith, don't let that distract you or cause you to lose your motivation. Value God's opinion more than other people's opinions, and choose to please God, no matter what others think.

- Invest your life in eternal purposes, remembering that only what Jesus does through you will last and that everything else (how much money you make, how famous you are, what possessions you have, how handsome or beautiful you are, etc.) will mean nothing in the light of eternity. Make your daily decisions according to what matters most to God. Always be willing to make the sacrifices necessary to share your faith as God leads you.

CONNECT WITH PEOPLE

- Find common interests with people you're trying to reach, and spend time together pursuing those interests. For example, if you and a co-worker both enjoy football, attend some games together. Or if you and a neighbor both like to create scrapbooks about your kids, take turns gathering at each other's houses to work on your scrapbooks together.

- As you talk with people and earn their trust, gradually and naturally direct your conversations toward spiritual issues. Know that if you build genuine friendships with people, they'll be motivated to hear what you have to say about Jesus.

- Pay attention to the divine appointments God brings your way, and don't hesitate to reach out to those people God leads you to reach out to – even if you've never met them before.

- Listen respectfully to people when they express spiritual views with which you disagree. Don't argue with them. Instead, let them fully express their thoughts and feelings, and then confidently and lovingly state your position.

- Write a personal reflection on a conflict you have had or are presently having with someone. Try to explain exactly how it arose in clear and objective terms. How can you be reconciled to this person in obedience to Romans 12:18? What may be holding you back? How can you overcome it?

SHOW PEOPLE HOW THE GOSPEL MEETS THEIR DEEPEST NEEDS

- Talk with people openly about their fear of death and how they can be assured of salvation. Let people know that, as Christians, they can have absolute assurance of eternal life beyond physical death. Help them understand that Earth is just a temporary home, but that life in heaven will last forever.

- Show people clearly how the Gospel is relevant to their lives and will give them the practical help they need every day. Let them know that they can apply its truths to their lives with confidence.

- Explain how the Gospel's truth is universal. Help people understand why the Bible is God's Word by discussing its fulfilled prophecies, historical evidence for its contents, the accuracy of how it presents the human condition, and its moral wisdom. Suggest turning to the Bible for guidance in every part of their lives.

- Encourage people to be reconciled to God through Jesus so they can then establish healthy and fulfilling relationships with others.

CREATE AND SHARE YOUR PERSONAL TESTIMONY

- Write down your personal testimony, summarizing: why you believed, when you believed, and the circumstances that brought you to faith. Keep your testimony simple and make sure it clearly communicates the Gospel message. Don't sensationalize your story; remember that you're trying to draw attention to Jesus rather than promoting yourself. Use the guidelines from *Becoming a God Magnet* to help you as you write (178-182).

- Practice telling your personal testimony to a friend, and get his or her feedback on how clearly you're communicating it and how well you're using it to present the Gospel message.

- Back up your testimony by living out your faith (treating people well, working hard, acting honestly, etc.) so others can see by your actions that you have integrity and that you mean what you say.

USE RESOURCES WELL

- Take advantage of resources such as New Testaments, copies of the Gospel of John, other books, tracts, CDs of worship music, videos, and other materials that can help you share God's message. But be sure not to rely on materials alone; don't neglect building genuine relationships with the people with whom you're sharing materials.

HELP PEOPLE GROW IN THEIR FAITH

- When people indicate that they want to explore faith further, consider inviting them to a worship service or event at your church, a Bible study or other small group, a course for seekers that explains the basics of Christianity (such as the Alpha Course), or a prayer ministry where people can pray about their needs with others.

- After someone begins a relationship with Jesus, do all you can to support them so they can grow in their faith. Encourage them to begin reading the Bible. Help them plug into a local church. Be available to meet with them regularly to pray, answer their questions, and study the Bible together.

- Remember to pray regularly for those to whom you have witnessed and those you have led to faith. Keep them lifted before God in prayer that they would grow spiritually and not falter in their faith. Pray for them to mature and become God Magnets themselves.

RESOURCES

Nicky Gumbel, *The Questions of Life, A Practical Introduction to the Christian Faith*, David C. Cook, 2002.

Dr. Paul Maier, *Jesus—Legend or Lord*, Available on DVD from tobiascom.com

Josh McDowell, *Evidence That Demands a Verdict*, Authentic Lifestyle, 2004.

Josh McDowell, *The New Evidence That Demands a Verdict, Fully Updated to Answer the Questions Challenging Christians Today*, Thomas Nelson, 1999.

Lee Strobel, *The Case for Christ: A Journalist's Personal Investigation of the Evidence for Jesus*, Zondervan, 1998.

Lee Strobel, The Case for a Creator: A Journalist Investigates Scientific Evidence That Points Toward God, Zondervan, 2005.

Lee Strobel, *The Case for Faith: A Journalist Investigates the Toughest Objections to Christianity*, Zondervan, 2000.

Stan Telchin, *Betrayed, Chosen*, revised edition, 2007.

For information on the Alpha course, visit www.alpha.org.

FOR GROUP LEADERS

Session One
INTRODUCTION: (Chapters 1–2)

The goal of this first study is to introduce the subject of evangelism using the conversion story of Harvey Katz in *Becoming a God Magnet* as well as a few Bible texts. It is important to encourage the group to discuss their feelings about sharing their faith and some of their misconceptions about God's part and their part in evangelizing others. Once people recognize they are called to faithfulness rather than numerical success, they can begin to relax. Then they are ready to learn what being a God Magnet is really all about.

Session Two:
IDENTIFICATION: *Speaking to the Heart* (Chapters 3–7)

This section will help group members discover the needs and desires inside people's hearts so they can reach out to them most effectively.

The key point to emphasize when discussing idols is that when people put other things in place of God, they can never give contentment because God is the only true source of contentment. The discontent that results from idols, however, creates an open door for the Gospel.

Listening is essential because it is a very simple yet powerful expression of unconditional love. So often we have failed to win people's trust because we are unwilling to pay the price to love them sincerely.

Praying for people who need the Lord means much more than asking God to save them. *Becoming a God Magnet* points out that prayer can also help us understand their needs and show love by identifying with them in their struggles.

Learning how to pray and listen to the Holy Spirit is crucial to reaching others for Christ. We must never forget that our job is not to save people, but to bear witness to the Gospel.

It is vital to determine each person's level of spiritual receptivity because that information alone should determine how we proceed and at what pace. This insight will help to alleviate people's fears about how to relate to people regarding spiritual topics.

Session Three:
PREPARATION: *You Are a Life Message* (Chapters 8–16)

This section helps group members develop lives that make them God Magnets--attracting people to Christ by the way they live. It focuses on how they can build godly character and invite the Holy Spirit to empower them.

As group leader, help each member to consider what it means when we say, "You are a Life Message," and ask what is each person's "life message"?

As your group discusses the various ways God works in our lives to help us grow in holiness, you can point out that God uses our struggles to achieve His good purposes, which in turn transform us into more effective witnesses for Christ.

Guide the group to see that God can heal the broken areas of our lives and then use the ways we have overcome in these areas to make us a great blessing to others. Rather than disqualifying us as effective witnesses, the transformation we undergo, by God's grace and power, can actually equip us for effective ministry.

Problems often seem confusing and frustrating when we are in the midst of them. This is where God's Word can speak to us clearly and show us what is really going on, if we will turn to the Lord for guidance. Lead the group in an understanding of how God uses His Word to guide us and to redirect our thinking and behavior. Encourage each one to be open to all the ways that God uses to make us more like Christ.

The portion of this section on being filled with the Holy Spirit could generate a lot of discussion. Don't allow those who have been filled with the Holy Spirit to judge or pressure those who have not been filled. Help the group to stay focused upon the fact that this is a wonderful gift God longs for us to have and experience.

If there are those who wish to be filled with the Holy Spirit, lead the group in a simple prayer over them or pray with them individually if you feel they would prefer this. Encourage them to trust God for their prayer language if it does not come right away.

Session Four:

PRESENTATION: *One Message, Many Methods* (Chapters 17–29)

This section looks at the many possible ways to share the single most life-changing message of all – the Gospel of Jesus Christ.

It's important that believers recognize they are not responsible to save people, but simply to bear witness. We also need to avoid pressuring people by recognizing that all we can do is help them to move on to the next stage in their journeys toward Christ.

The Gospel is urgent news because everyone has sinned and needs God's forgiveness to be saved from eternal judgment. We know that Jesus Christ is the Way, the Truth and the Life, and without Him, no one will see heaven. As believers, we will also face a time of accounting when our works are examined to see if we deserve a reward in heaven. It is important to distinguish between the concept of a reward for faithful service and earning your way into heaven through good works.

You can help your group members understand that sharing Christ can fit into the flow of their daily lives if they relax, get to know people, and stay open to the Lord's leading.

As your group discusses the reality of death, you can guide them to talk about how presenting the promise of eternal life will motivate people to consider the Gospel.

Since people from many different religious and cultural backgrounds surround us, it is vital that we understand how to present the Gospel clearly to people who are different from us. Encourage lots of discussion on this question based upon people's experiences.

Help your group members discuss key points about the Gospel message, its relevance to real life, and how to begin communicating these to friends and acquaintances. Encourage them to think through some reasonable responses to nonbelievers' questions about the Bible's truthfulness and authority. Suggest that the members of your group consider how the Gospel transforms their relationships with others.

When your group discusses how to issue invitations and deal with arguments, emphasize showing respect for people's choices and feelings, refusing to use pressure and maintaining a gentle and humble spirit.

You can help group members understand the great value of their personal testimonies. Urge them to write their testimonies down. Consider having one or two group members share their testimonies spontaneously in the group with the understanding that they will keep it to a maximum of three to five minutes.

As the group leader, you can suggest some practical resources that group members can use to share their faith. If possible, have some copies of these resources available for the group to browse or purchase. You may wish to suggest that the group continue to meet after you all have completed studying *Becoming a God Magnet* to study one of the resources suggested at the end of this guide.

Conclude with a summary of what people have learned and any relevant praise reports on winning others to Christ, and then close in prayer.

Harvey Katz

BECOMING A GOD MAGNET
Life Lessons In Sharing Your Faith

If you've ever had your heart pound as you opened your mouth to share your faith . . . this book is for you!

Many Christians view evangelism as a chore, a responsibility they dread. Harvey Katz has good news: God wants to attract people to Jesus Christ through your life . . . in a relaxed, natural, joyful way. In this book, Harvey Katz will show you how.

Mary Haskett

REVEREND MOTHER'S DAUGHTER
A Real Life Story

In this gripping account, the author shares her personal story of racial rejection, physical and sexual abuse, and wartime trauma. Through it all, she is aware of a driving force in her life that ultimately brings her to Jesus Christ.

Howard Katz

SEVEN ESSENTIAL RELATIONSHIPS
How To Pass God's Crucial Tests

The author uses the seven stages in the creation of a clay vessel, as well as an exposition of the life of Joseph, to illustrate each of the seven crucial tests that every believer must pass.

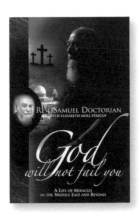

Rev. Samuel Doctorian
with Elizabeth Moll Stalcup, Ph.D.

GOD WILL NOT FAIL YOU
A Life of Miracles in the Middle East and Beyond

The miraculous life story of Rev. Samuel Doctorian, the renowned evangelist used mightily by God in the Middle East and around the world.

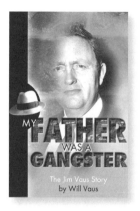

Will Vaus

MY FATHER WAS A GANGSTER
The Jim Vaus Story

One of the most fascinating conversion stories of the 20th century—the dramatic life story of Jim Vaus, former associate to America's underworld.

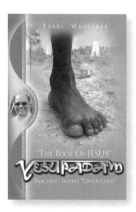

Terri Whitaker

YESUPADAM
Reaching India's Untouched

Yesupadam is the amazing story of God's miraculous work through an Untouchable Indian believer in Jesus and his Love-n-Care ministry in eastern India.

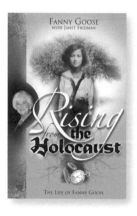

Fanny Goose
with Janet Fridman

RISING FROM THE HOLOCAUST
The Life of Fanny Goose

The astonishing real life story of an indomitable young Jewish girl who miraculously survives the horrors of Hitler's plot to destroy her people and goes on to live a joyful life.

Major General Jerry R. Curry

FROM PRIVATE TO GENERAL

*An African American Soldier
Rises Through the Ranks*

Major General Jerry Curry vividly describes his life journey of military missions, powerful positions, and his relationship with the true source of authority—his Father in heaven.

Charlene Curry

THE GENERAL'S LADY

God's Faithfulness to a Military Spouse

Charlene Curry recounts all the joys and challenges of being a career military spouse and how she triumphed over difficulties by relying on a source of spiritual power that transformed her life.

Fern C. Willner

WHEN FAITH IS ENOUGH

*A Safari of Destiny that Reveals
Principles to Live By*

A faith-inspiring story of a missionary wife and mother of seven relying completely on God in the heart of Africa.